BATHROOM SIGNS

BATHROOM SIGNS

WEIRD, WACKY AND SOMETIMES WARPED
PLACES TO FIND RELIEF I.P. DAILY

imagine!
Publishing

An Imagine Book
Published by Charlesbridge
85 Main Street, Watertown, MA 02472
(617) 926-0329
www.charlesbridge.com

Library of Congress Cataloging-in-Publication Data available
ISBN 978-1-936140-31-2

Printed in China, January, 2011

2 4 6 8 10 9 7 5 3 1

For information about custom editions, special sales,
premium and corporate purchases, please contact
Charlesbridge Publishing at specialsales@charlesbridge.com

CONTENTS

2P

INTRODUCTION

No matter where you go in the world, there are four little words that you absolutely need to know. You can get away with forgetting "Hello, my name is..." or "Where are you from?" but you'll be up a creek if you can't say: "Where is the bathroom?"

Anticipating this universal need, helpful restaurant owners, park guides, and tourism boards have erected signs that breach language barriers and also provide some helpful hints about local customs. Did you know that in many parts of the world, for example, people squat rather than sit on the toilet seat? Or that in some areas, public restrooms can only be used in case of emergency?

This eye-opening, jaw-dropping collection of bathroom signs from around the world will leave you laughing out loud. But if you happen to be reading in a public restroom, try to restrain your mirth: the people on the other side of the stall can hear you.

LOCATION, LOCATION, LOCATION

Every time you leave home for more than a few hours, whether you're traveling a few miles or a thousand, some part of your brain is always in surveillance mode for bathroom signs. When nature isn't calling, you can afford to be choosy. Which bathrooms are the cleanest? The safest? Closest to your favorite coffee stand? On the other hand, finding a place to go when you *really* need to go can be physically painful and mentally distressing. When that happens, a simple, ordinary bathroom sign—that small, universally recognized indicator that relief is just around the corner—may well be the most welcome sign in the world.

LAST PUBLIC

TOILETS

BEFORE

FRANCE

RESTROOM

THERE ARE NO
RESTROOMS
AT THE BOTTOM
OF THE GORGE

SPORTS MASSAGE
FUN RUN ENTRIES
HEALTHY BREAKFAST
FUN RUN START
CORPORATE TENT
10K ATHLETE ASSEMBLY
TOILETS
FIRST AID

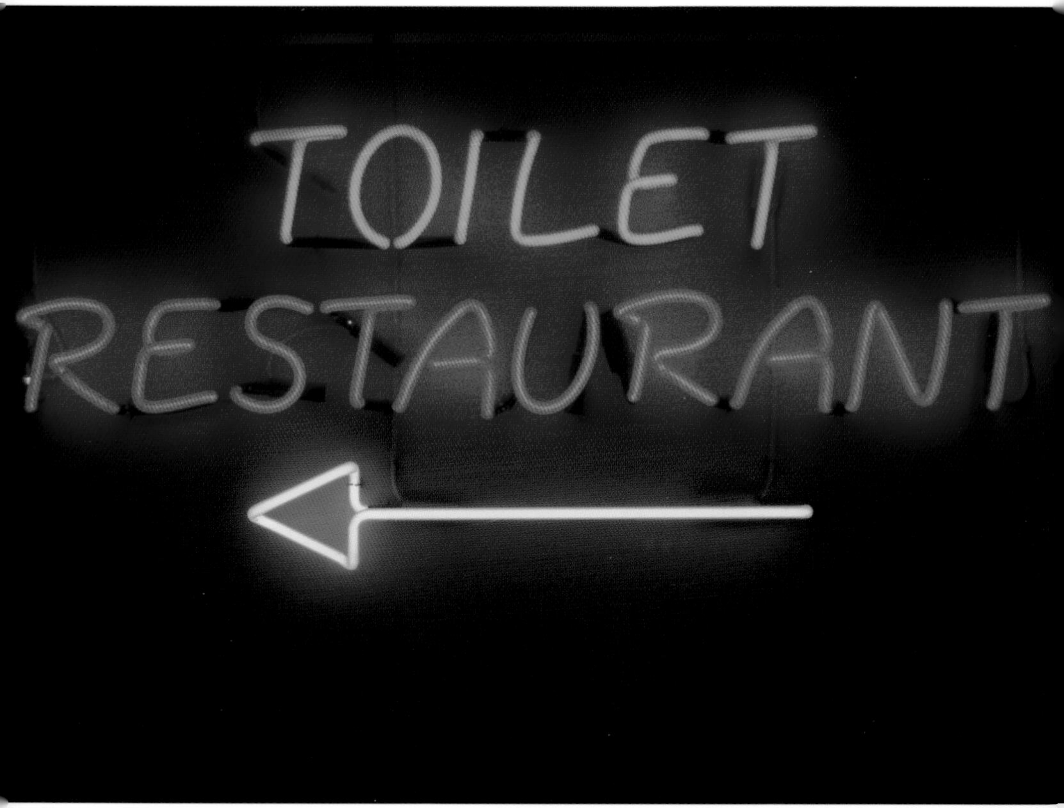
TOILET
RESTAURANT

To the Toilets
Co-Ordinates
S 24 50 731
E 16 58 768

25

CLEAN REST ROOMS

1000 FEET

28

SUPER LOO

32

NEW ZEALAND

4U2P

⚓ HOME OF THE AMERICA'S CUP ⚓

GENTS

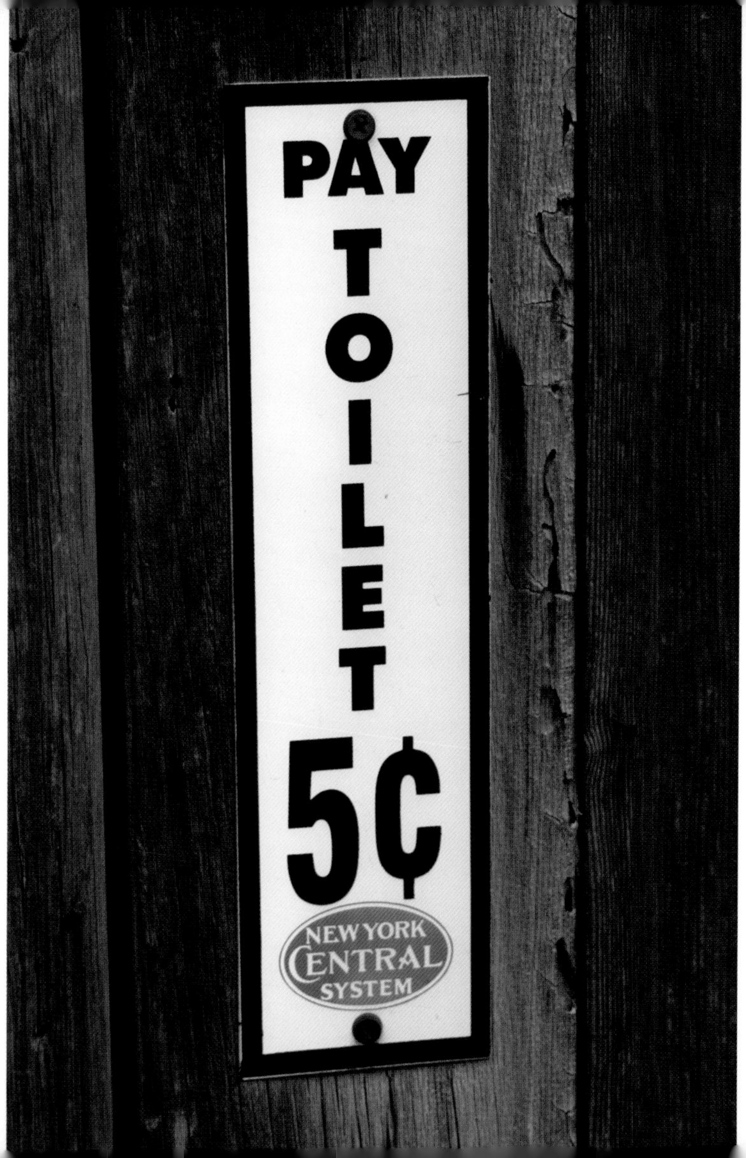
PAY
TOILET
5¢
NEW YORK
CENTRAL
SYSTEM

CAUGHT SHORT
IN WESTMINSTER?

Text **TOILET** to **80097**
to locate your nearest public toilet.

Texts are charged at 25p

le pissoir

43

45

men

women

man

woman

SITTERS 👉

👈 STANDERS

64

WOMEN   WC   MEN

65

御婦人用 殿方用

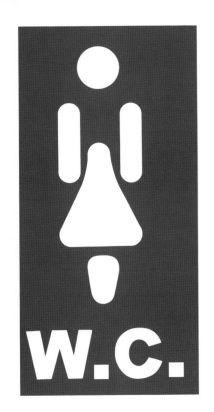

W.C.

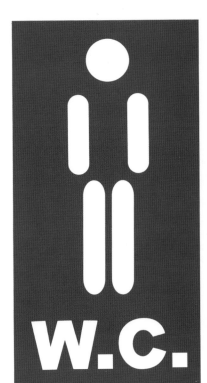

W.C.

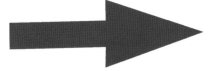

HOMMES

FEMMES

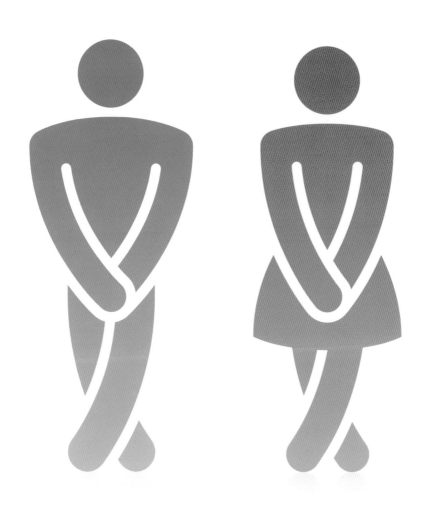

74

Ladies

Gentlemen

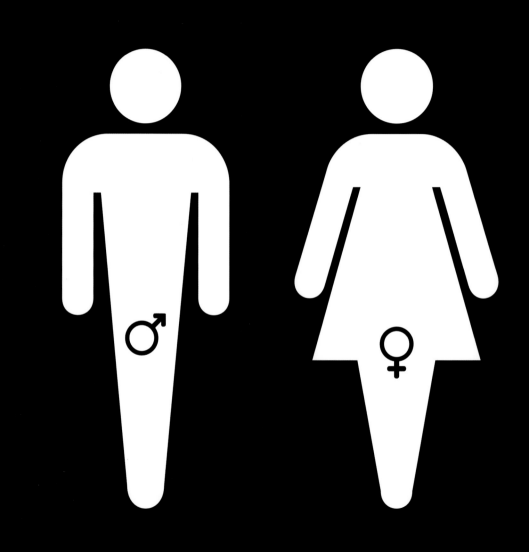

TOILETTE

TOILETTE

Toilet

Once again, make sure that you are a woman.

This is a female-only toilet.

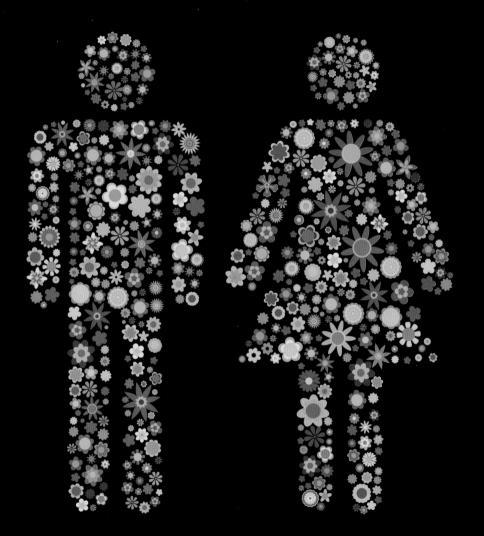

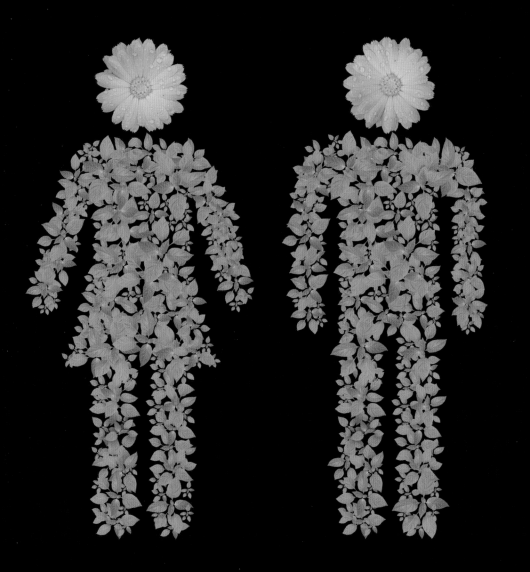

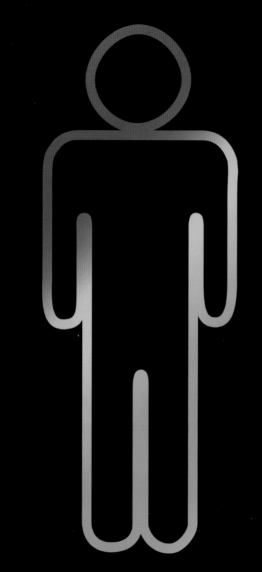

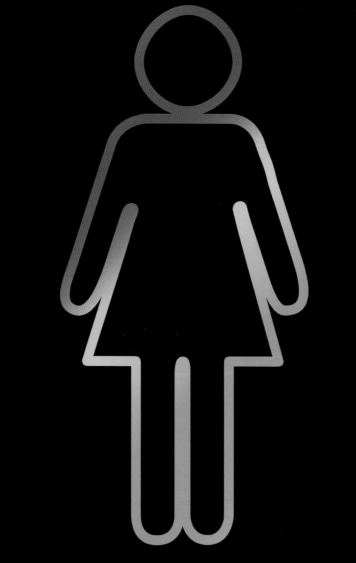

LADIES

GENTLEMEN

TOILET

GO WITH THE FLOW

While practices vary around the world, children are typically potty trained by the time they're entering preschool. It would appear, however, that many people need a little remedial work on this important skill. Some people need reminders to improve their aim, so to speak, or clear instructions on where to position different body parts (no feet on the seat or heads in the bowl, please). Others need a refresher course on bathroom equipment: that small, porcelain bowl with two handles and a faucet—that's for washing hands. The larger bowl with the handle? That's the place you do your business. When in the bathroom, it's important to remember that safety comes first: please put down your firearms.

TOILET

FOR SAFETY AND
MAINTENANCE REASONS,
PLEASE DO NOT STAND ON
THE TOILET SEATS.

TOILET

101

102

103

HOLD
for
effective
flush.

FLUSH

BEFORE AND AFTER USE

PLEASE
DO NOT
COMPACT
BY HAND

108

GIRLS

LADIES!

Someone broke
the lock.

Block the door
with your foot.

PLEASE DO NOT STEAL OUR TOILET PAPER! WE WILL GLADLY SELL YOU A ROLL IF YOU'RE DESPERATE.

(YES, THIS HAS BECOME A REAL PROBLEM!)

This is NOT a reading room. Those who OFTEN wait somewhat patiently for the restroom to be free would appreciate it if everyone would keep that in mind.

THANK YOU.

SOUTHERN RAILWAY

GENTLEMEN

PLEASE ADJUST YOUR
DRESS BEFORE LEAVING

WATERLOO STATION   19211

Push to Flush

Do Not Flush while Seated

DO NOT HANDLE YOUR FIREARM IN THE RESTROOM

Leave your gun in the holster and remove the holster from your belt.

120

Please use the restrooms to go potty, NOT this closet!

←----

CHI
TIEU

URINATE ONLY
(Make Water Piss Only)

Toilets are for

Emergency

Use Only

DIVERSIONS & PERVERSIONS

Once that stall door closes, it's private time. Or is it? Some use the sanctuary of the stall for solitary pursuits, such as perusing a magazine, reading a book, or perhaps even doing a crossword puzzle. Others use the downtime for getting some chores done: the toilet rim can be just the spot to clean off those mud-caked boots you've been clomping around in. Then there are those who find the privacy well suited to more, shall we say, social interactions: if you're creative and limber enough, a bathroom stall can be the perfect spot to get to know someone much, much better. If you do happen to accomplish such a feat, though, please don't use the toilet as an ashtray afterward.

4 ACROSS CLUES

9 Self-admirer is to get awkward.(7)
11 In petrol, it represents a unit.(5)
13 Want plague round Romania.(6)
18 Awfully dry in Hants? An answer!(8)
22 Not observed since the finale?(4,5)
25 Evening work at the laundry.(7)
27 Midas touch for a rich send-off?(6,9)

4 DOWN CLUES

2 Small worker is a speed-writer.(9)
4 Don't start brawling to get a trip.(6)
6 Silly Nigel, toff, is careless.(9)
8 Starts up the motor and attacks.(5,2)
16 Paradise: sharing all endlessly.(7-2)
18 A share of assistance.(7)
21 Salt from the ocean, boy.(6)
24 Negative amount in sum altered.(5)

1 At a W-town tan tons refused.(5,3,4,3)
10 Less generous when more drunk.(7)
12 Flower of reflective youth.(9)
15 Norse Dan created a shelter.(6)
19 Narrow, but said to be honest.(6)
24 Rock from dons with little gravity.(5)
26 Dawn is nurse, retrained. (7)

1 Like a car, went free - no engine!(7)
3 400 in top hotel, it emerges.(5)
5 Call for a drunken English clique.(8)
7 Messages written in music.(6)
14 Happen to exude moisture.(9)
17 Where learner swam to. (2,6)
20 Circus swing with catchability?(7)
23 Reel back the rings.(5)

5 ACROSS CLUES

1 Rustic grabs hen's head for game.(6)
10 The maiden provides help.(4)

6 State an Inn inside a monument!(6)

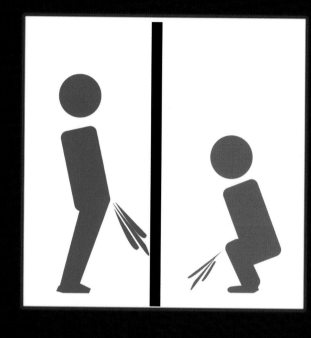

TOILET

TOILET

MEN

BIOHAZARD

134

WOMEN

 BIOHAZARD

TOILET

WOMEN

**PLEASE
NO DOGS ALLOWED
IN RESTROOMS
AT ANY TIME**

139

NO PEEKING!

Use of Cameras
Or Video Recorders
Of Any Type Is
Prohibited
In This Area

MEN

BIG DADDY'S HOUSE OF RELIEF

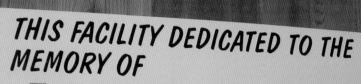

THIS FACILITY DEDICATED TO THE
MEMORY OF
JOHN J. CRAPPER
INVENTED 1914
Thanks for the Convenience

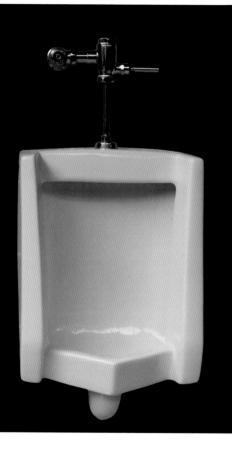

EXPRESS
LANE

2 BEERS
OR
LESS

TAP PROVIDED
TO
CLEAN BOOTS

DO NOT USE
TOILETS

NEVER SQUAT
WITH YOUR SPURS ON

ONLY ONE BUTT IS ALLOWED IN THIS CUBICLE

INTERNATIONAL TOILETS

GOING IN: *Russian*

INSIDE: *European*

COMING OUT: *Finnish*

TO THE SHORT BLONDE WHO
STRADDLES THE TOILET WHEN YOU PEE,

(you know who you are ... you have
small feet and wear heels all the time)

PLEASE WIPE YOUR PEE OFF THE SEAT!!!!

IT'S DISGUSTING AND
YOU LEAVE SOME EVERY TIME!!!!!!!

150

NICE ASS

We'd like you to keep it that way
so we have installed hygienic,
disinfectant wipes for you to clean
the toilet seat before each use.

Enjoy your visit and remember
no job is finished until the
paperwork is done.

151

This potty is lazy. please
 make sure it
flushes all the
way so presents aren't left
for others.

We all thank you!

If you happen to leave a little slush, please push the button for an extra flush.

Thank you for being considerate.

MALES

Our AIM is to Keep
Our Bathroom CLEAN.
Your Aim
Would be Deeply
APPRECIATED.

Any Questions???
Ask LORRAINA

PLEASE ONLY TAKE AN
EMERGENCY SHIT IN THESE
TOILETS. PEE ONLY.

159

ACKNOWLEDGMENTS...

The author would like to thank the following photographers for kindly sharing their images of bathroom signs: Matthew Abbott (page 38), Gary Albrecht (page 110), Aaron Evans (page 37), Colin Grey (page 154), Lloyd Gross (pages 31, 68, and 69), Ronald Ham (page 111), Graham Laurence (page 138), Benny Lin (page 41), Kathy Nobles (page 6), Lois Ronberg (page 149), Jonathan Sharp (page 147), Victoria Shephard (page 143), and Amanda Vincent-Rous (page 40).